The Wealth Accelerator

From Financial Literacy To Fastlane Freedom

The Wealth Accelerator: From Financial Literacy to Fastlane Freedom
Copyright © 2024 Jonathan Cross
All rights reserved.

No part of this book may be reproduced, distributed, or transmitted in any form or by any means, including photocopying, recording, or other electronic or mechanical methods, without the prior written permission of the author, except in the case of brief quotations embodied in critical reviews and certain other noncommercial uses permitted by copyright law.

ISBN: 9798344690032

Disclaimer

This book is intended to provide helpful and informative material on the subjects addressed. It is provided with the understanding that the author is not engaged in rendering legal, financial, or other professional advice. Readers should consult a professional where appropriate. The author and publisher specifically disclaim any liability that is incurred from the use or application of the contents of this book.

Printed in the United States of America

Second Edition

Preface

In a world where financial security often feels like a distant dream, many people follow outdated advice —work hard, save a little, and hope for the best. But in reality, this traditional approach to wealth-building doesn't lead to financial freedom. It's slow, restrictive, and leaves you vulnerable to economic changes and unforeseen setbacks.

I've seen firsthand how the right knowledge, mindset, and strategy can accelerate wealth creation. This book is the culmination of my experiences and insights on breaking free from the limiting beliefs around money and taking control of your financial future.

The Wealth Accelerator: From Financial Literacy to Fastlane Freedom is about rethinking how you approach wealth. It's designed to give you the tools to move beyond the "Slowlane" of working for a paycheck, saving for decades, and hoping to retire comfortably. Instead, you'll learn how to build assets, create multiple income streams, and fast-track your way to financial independence—while enjoying life along the way.

This book is a blueprint for those who want to accelerate their wealth-building journey. Whether you're just starting out or already on your path, these principles will help you take control of your financial destiny.

My hope is that by the time you finish reading, you'll have the knowledge and confidence to design your own wealth accelerator—and the freedom to live life on your terms.

Introduction:
The Broken Financial Script

Most people are handed a flawed financial script when they step into adulthood—a script that's outdated and keeps them trapped in a cycle of work, stress, and limited financial progress. We are taught to believe that the key to wealth is working hard, saving diligently, and hoping for a comfortable retirement in the distant future. But in reality, this "slow and steady" approach is ineffective for the majority. While it offers a sense of security, it often leads to financial stagnation and dissatisfaction.

Instead of building wealth and achieving freedom, many are caught in the rat race, barely staying afloat as the cost of living rises and unexpected expenses, layoffs, or economic downturns hit. The traditional method—let's call it the "Slowlane"—is not only slow but fundamentally flawed. It relies on decades of saving a portion of your income, all the while hoping that external factors like inflation or market fluctuations don't undermine your efforts. Even in the best-case scenario, the "reward" at the end is the promise of a comfortable retirement, often long after your prime years are behind you.

But what if there's a faster, more effective way to achieve financial freedom? One that doesn't require sacrificing your best years for the faint hope of a distant future? This book is about rethinking wealth creation entirely. It's about embracing an approach I call the "Fastlane"—a method that focuses on building wealth efficiently through asset creation, financial literacy, and strategic action, all while enjoying the journey along the way.

Chapter 1:

Redefining Wealth:

Mindset Over Money

When people think of wealth, they often picture luxury—expensive cars, large estates, and extravagant lifestyles. But wealth is much more than material possessions. True wealth is a mindset, a way of life, and a set of principles that guide how you grow and manage your resources. It's about freedom, security, and the ability to live life on your terms.

Most people measure wealth by their income, net worth, or the value of their assets, but this approach often leads to a misguided pursuit. They work harder, chase higher salaries, and acquire more possessions, believing that more money will bring them happiness. But this way of thinking overlooks the most important aspect of wealth—freedom. True wealth isn't about how much you have but about how much control you have over your time and your life.

Wealth as Freedom

At its core, wealth is about freedom—the freedom to live without the constant pressure of trading your time for money. It's about creating financial independence where your income isn't tied to the hours you work, giving you the ability to pursue passions, explore opportunities, and make choices without the constraint of financial worry.

This kind of freedom can only be achieved by shifting from a scarcity mindset—where you focus on limitations and fear of loss—to an abundance mindset, where you focus on possibilities and growth. Most people operate under the belief that wealth is scarce and that opportunities for financial independence are limited. This mentality holds them back from taking risks, making investments, and adopting the strategies necessary to build true wealth.

The Scarcity vs. Abundance Mindset

The scarcity mindset is rooted in fear—fear of not having enough money, fear of failure, and fear of taking risks. This mindset encourages hoarding resources, playing it safe, and avoiding opportunities for growth. People with a scarcity mindset stay stuck in jobs they don't enjoy, afraid to step out of their comfort zones. They think small, save cautiously, and often see financial success as something that only happens to the lucky or privileged.

In contrast, the abundance mindset focuses on growth, opportunity, and creation. People with an abundance mentality believe that wealth is limitless and that there are countless opportunities to create value and generate income. They understand that money is a tool, not the goal, and that true wealth comes from creating value for others, not simply accumulating possessions.

By adopting an abundance mindset, you can begin to see that wealth isn't something that happens to you—it's something you create. It's a mindset shift from earning money to building assets, from working for others to owning and creating value.

Building Assets, Not Just Income

One of the key shifts in redefining wealth is focusing on assets instead of just income. While most people believe that increasing their salary is the path to wealth, this is a limiting approach. If your income is tied to your time, there's only so much you can earn because there are only so many hours in the day.

True wealth comes from building assets—things that generate income independently of your time. Assets can include businesses, real estate, intellectual property, and investments. By building assets, you create streams of income that flow to you whether or not you're actively working. This is the difference between linear income (earned from working) and passive income (earned from assets).

For example, consider someone with a job that pays $80,000 a year. This income is tied directly to their time. Now, imagine that same person owns rental properties generating $1,500 per month in passive income. While their job requires constant effort, the rental income continues to flow even if they're not working. The more assets you build, the closer you get to financial independence.

The Importance of Leverage

Another critical aspect of wealth-building is leverage —the ability to multiply your efforts through the use of other people's time, money, or resources. Leverage can take many forms:

- **Financial Leverage:** Using other people's money (such as loans or investments) to grow your assets faster than you could with your own money alone.
- **Time Leverage:** Utilizing systems, technology, or employees to multiply your efforts so that your income doesn't depend entirely on your time.

- **Technology Leverage:** Leveraging technology to scale your business or investments, allowing you to generate income without needing to increase your workload.

Leverage is what allows you to create exponential growth in your wealth, rather than the slow, incremental gains of traditional employment.

Wealth is Measured in Time, Not Just Money

True wealth is measured not just by how much money you have but by how much control you have over your time. Financial independence means that your passive income exceeds your living expenses, allowing you to live life on your terms without the need to trade time for money.

This redefinition of wealth is the foundation for building lasting financial freedom. It's about creating assets, leveraging your resources, and shifting your mindset from scarcity to abundance. By doing so, you begin the journey toward a future of security, freedom, and true wealth.

Lessons Learned:

- Wealth is not just about money; it's a mindset shift focused on building assets and financial independence.
- True wealth means having control over your time, options, and life choices.
- Financial literacy is the foundation for long-term wealth-building.
- A wealth-building mindset requires discipline, delayed gratification, and a long-term perspective.

Chapter 2:

The Asset-Building Formula

Building wealth is not solely about earning more; it's about accumulating assets that grow over time and generate value. Assets are the key to creating long-term wealth, and understanding the types of assets available and how to acquire them is essential for accelerating your path to financial freedom.

What Are Assets?

An asset is anything that adds value or generates income over time. This can include investments, property, businesses, or intellectual property. In contrast, liabilities take money out of your pocket without adding value. To build wealth, your focus should be on acquiring assets while minimizing liabilities.

There are three primary types of assets you can build to increase your net worth:

1. **Income-Generating Assets**: Assets that produce cash flow, such as rental properties, dividend-paying stocks, or businesses.

2. **Appreciating Assets**: Assets that increase in value over time, like real estate, art, or stocks.
3. **Intangible Assets**: Intellectual property, such as books, patents, or trademarks, that can be monetized.

The Asset-Building Formula:

1. **Start with Financial Literacy**: Understanding how money works is the foundation. Without a clear grasp of how to manage, invest, and grow money, you will struggle to build lasting wealth.

2. **Establish an Emergency Fund**: Before diving into investing, ensure you have a safety net. An emergency fund helps you avoid high-interest debt when unexpected expenses arise.

3. **Save and Invest Regularly**: The key to growing wealth is consistency. Regularly set aside money from your income and invest it in appreciating or income-generating assets.

4. **Acquire Assets That Appreciate**: Invest in assets that not only produce income but also grow in value over time. This could include real estate, stocks, or businesses.

5. **Reinvest Profits**: As your assets begin to generate income, reinvest that income to acquire more assets or expand your current holdings.

6. **Leverage for Growth**: Use tools like good debt, partnerships, and automation to scale your asset base. This can accelerate your journey to financial freedom.

Illustration: Steps to Financial Freedom

Here is a visual representation of the steps to financial freedom, which demonstrates how each stage builds upon the previous one to create a sustainable wealth-building strategy.

The pyramid begins with **Financial Literacy**, moves through **Savings and Investments**, **Asset Building**, and culminates with **Multiple Income Streams** and **Entrepreneurship**. This visual guide provides an overview of how to structure your wealth-building journey, focusing on gradual progression.

When it comes to creating lasting wealth, the key is building assets—not simply increasing income. While most people focus on earning a higher paycheck or getting promotions, this strategy will only take you so far. True financial independence isn't built on income alone, but on accumulating and growing assets that generate wealth independently of your time and effort.

As stated above, an asset is anything that puts money into your pocket, either by generating income or appreciating in value. The more assets you own, the more you can grow your wealth without the need to trade time for money.

Assets vs. Liabilities: Know the Difference

One of the most common mistakes people make is confusing assets with liabilities. A liability is something that takes money out of your pocket, while an asset adds to your wealth. For example, a personal home may feel like an asset, but it is often a liability because it requires ongoing maintenance, taxes, and upkeep, and doesn't generate income unless you sell it or rent it out.

In contrast, a rental property that produces positive cash flow is a true asset. It generates income every month, adding to your financial independence rather than depleting your resources. Understanding the difference between assets and liabilities is the first step to building lasting wealth.

The Power of Compound Growth

Compound growth is one of the most powerful forces in wealth-building. When you invest in assets that appreciate in value or generate recurring income, your returns begin to compound over time.

Compounding allows your money to grow exponentially, not linearly.

Consider this: If you invest $10,000 at an annual return of 7%, after the first year, your investment will be worth $10,700. In the second year, you'll earn 7% on the new balance of $10,700, and so on. Over time, this compounding effect leads to significant growth with minimal additional effort.

Compounding doesn't just apply to financial investments. It can apply to businesses, real estate, and intellectual property. The longer you allow your assets to grow, the more powerful compounding becomes. This is why it's crucial to start building assets as early as possible.

Types of Assets You Should Build

Now that you understand the importance of building assets, let's explore the different types you can accumulate to grow your wealth.

1. **Real Estate:** Rental properties, commercial real estate, or land investments are some of the most popular and effective wealth-building assets. Real estate provides a combination of cash flow from rental income and appreciation over time. Plus, it offers tax advantages such as depreciation deductions.

2. **Stocks and Bonds:** Owning shares of profitable companies or investing in government or corporate bonds is another effective way to build assets. Stocks offer potential for both dividends and capital gains, while bonds provide more stability through regular interest payments.

3. **Businesses:** Owning a business can be one of the most powerful wealth-building strategies. Whether you start your own or invest in someone else's, businesses allow you to scale your efforts and generate income without being tied to your time. A well-run business creates leverage, allowing you to grow wealth rapidly.

4. **Intellectual Property:** Books, patents, and software are examples of intellectual property that can generate passive income. Once created, intellectual property can continue to bring in revenue without requiring further time or effort from you.

By building a diverse portfolio of assets—across real estate, businesses, stocks, and intellectual property—you can grow your wealth exponentially over time, reducing your reliance on any single source of income.

Leverage: Multiplying Your Wealth-Building Potential

Leverage is a powerful tool for accelerating your asset growth. It allows you to use other people's money, time, or resources to achieve far greater results than you could on your own.

- **Financial Leverage:** By using loans or investor capital, you can acquire more assets than you could with just your own money. For example, using a mortgage to buy a rental property allows you to control a larger asset for a smaller down payment.

- **Time Leverage:** Hiring employees or using automation systems allows you to multiply your efforts without needing to work more hours. This is especially important for business owners who want to scale their operations.

- **Technology Leverage:** With advancements in technology, you can now scale businesses, investments, and systems much faster than ever before. From automated marketing tools to investment platforms, technology provides endless opportunities to leverage your efforts.

The combination of building assets and using leverage is the foundation of rapid wealth-building. It allows you to scale your income and grow your wealth much faster than the traditional "work and save" model.

Lessons Learned:

- Income is important, but building and accumulating assets is key to true wealth.
- Assets generate value and income over time, whereas liabilities drain your financial resources.
- Invest in appreciating assets such as real estate, stocks, or businesses to grow your wealth over time.
- Create multiple asset streams to diversify and secure financial independence.

Chapter 3:

Escape the Paycheck Trap

For most people, financial security is tied to a steady paycheck. From a young age, we're taught that success means landing a stable job, climbing the corporate ladder, and saving for retirement. But this paycheck mentality often leads to a dangerous trap—a cycle where your entire financial well-being is tied to your job, leaving you vulnerable to job loss, economic downturns, and burnout.

In this chapter, we'll explore how to escape the paycheck trap by building income streams that don't rely on trading time for money. This shift in mindset will allow you to create wealth that works for you, even when you're not working.

The Illusion of Job Security

Many people believe that a steady paycheck provides security. However, relying on a single source of income—your job—can actually be very risky. Economic changes, company restructuring, or health issues can all disrupt your job and your income. The

COVID-19 pandemic, for example, showed just how quickly job security can disappear.

True financial security comes from diversifying your income streams. By building multiple sources of income, you can reduce your dependence on any one job or paycheck, giving yourself more control over your financial future.

The Limitations of Trading Time for Money

In the traditional job model, you trade time for money. No matter how high your salary or hourly rate, your earning potential is limited by the number of hours in a day. This means that you'll always face a ceiling on your income unless you learn to build income streams that don't require your constant effort.

Passive income, on the other hand, allows you to earn money even when you're not actively working. This could come from rental income, dividends, royalties, or automated businesses. The key to escaping the paycheck trap is learning to build these streams of passive income, so that your financial security is no longer dependent on your time.

What is Passive Income?

Passive income is income that continues to flow even when you're not actively working. It comes from assets or systems that generate money without requiring your direct involvement. Examples of passive income include:

- **Rental Properties:** Income from tenants paying rent, providing a steady stream of cash flow.
- **Dividend Stocks:** Regular payouts from your investments in profitable companies.
- **Royalties:** Payments for intellectual property, such as books, music, or inventions.
- **Online Businesses:** Automated e-commerce or affiliate marketing businesses that generate sales with minimal input from you.

By building streams of passive income, you create financial security that isn't tied to a paycheck or your time. The goal is to accumulate enough passive income to cover your living expenses, allowing you to live life on your terms.

Building Multiple Income Streams

One of the best ways to protect yourself from financial instability is to create multiple streams of income. Instead of relying on one paycheck, diversify your income sources through investments, businesses, real estate, and other assets. This diversification reduces your financial risk and increases your earning potential.

Think of it like building a financial safety net—if one stream of income dries up, you have others to rely on. This gives you the freedom to take risks, explore new opportunities, and build wealth more effectively.

Entrepreneurship: The Ultimate Paycheck Trap Escape

Starting your own business is one of the most powerful ways to escape the paycheck trap. Entrepreneurship allows you to build an income-generating asset that doesn't rely on your time or effort alone. By building scalable systems and leveraging employees or technology, you can grow your business exponentially, generating income without being tied to a job.

As an entrepreneur, you control your income potential. There are no salary caps, no corporate hierarchies, and no limits on what you can achieve. While entrepreneurship comes with its risks, it also offers the greatest potential for financial freedom and independence.

Lessons Learned:

- Relying solely on a paycheck limits your financial growth and keeps you in the "rat race."
- Transitioning from trading time for money to building income streams that work for you is essential.
- Financial freedom comes from breaking the paycheck-to-paycheck cycle and focusing on building passive income.
- Start by managing expenses, increasing savings, and diverting funds toward income-generating investments.

Chapter 4:

The Fastlane Paradigm Shift

There are two primary ways people pursue wealth: the traditional **Slowlane** and the transformative **Fastlane**. Most people follow the Slowlane, the approach that tells us to work hard, save diligently, and slowly accumulate wealth over decades. This method may eventually lead to a comfortable retirement, but it's often a long, frustrating journey.

In contrast, the Fastlane represents a completely different mindset—one that focuses on accelerating financial success through strategic actions. It's not about waiting until you're 60 or 70 to enjoy life. Instead, the Fastlane allows you to achieve financial freedom while you're still young enough to make the most of it.

This chapter explores how adopting a Fastlane mentality can transform your financial future and lead to faster, more impactful wealth creation.

The Slowlane: A Path of Delayed Gratification

The Slowlane is built on traditional financial wisdom: get a good job, save a percentage of your income, invest in safe assets like mutual funds or retirement accounts, and over the course of several decades, compound interest will grow your wealth. This approach emphasizes long-term saving, delayed gratification, and security over risk.

However, the Slowlane has significant drawbacks:

- **Limited Growth:** Your income is directly tied to the number of hours you work, placing a cap on your earnings.
- **Dependence on External Factors:** Job security, market conditions, and inflation are factors you cannot control, yet they can have a massive impact on your wealth-building efforts.

- **Time Sacrifice:** You spend your most productive years working hard, only to enjoy wealth and freedom later in life, assuming everything goes according to plan.

While the Slowlane may work for some, it requires a significant time investment and offers limited flexibility. The biggest flaw is that it delays freedom until later in life, when energy and opportunities may be diminished.

The Fastlane: A Shift Toward Exponential Growth

The Fastlane challenges traditional thinking. Instead of focusing on saving slowly over decades, it's about taking bold, leveraged actions to build wealth more quickly. The Fastlane encourages entrepreneurship, value creation, and building scalable systems that allow your income to grow exponentially, not linearly.

The core principles of the Fastlane include:

- **Leverage:** Instead of trading time for money, the Fastlane emphasizes leveraging systems, people, and technology to multiply your efforts.
- **Value Creation:** Wealth is built by solving problems and creating value for others. The more value you create, the more wealth you generate.
- **Scaling:** In the Fastlane, growth isn't incremental—it's exponential. By building scalable businesses or investments, you can accelerate your wealth-building process.

The Fastlane isn't about working harder; it's about working smarter. It's about building systems that generate income and wealth even when you're not actively involved.

Why the Fastlane Works

The Fastlane works because it capitalizes on two powerful concepts: leverage and scale. When you leverage other people's time, money, and resources, you can achieve far more than you ever could alone. And when you build systems that scale—whether it's a business, an investment portfolio, or intellectual property—you create the opportunity for exponential growth.

For example, consider a traditional job where your income is tied to your hours worked. No matter how skilled you are, there's a limit to how much you can earn. Now, imagine you own an e-commerce business that sells products online. Once the systems are in place (automated ordering, customer service, fulfillment), the business can generate sales 24/7, without requiring your active involvement. That's the power of scale and leverage at work.

The Fastlane allows you to create wealth faster and more efficiently by building income streams that don't require constant effort. It's about creating systems that grow your wealth while freeing up your time.

The Risk of Playing It Safe

Many people are hesitant to embrace the Fastlane because they fear risk. The Slowlane feels safer—it offers the comfort of a steady paycheck and the promise of future security. But in reality, the Slowlane is often more risky because it depends on factors outside your control (e.g., job stability, market performance).

In contrast, the Fastlane encourages calculated risk-taking. Entrepreneurs and investors understand that while there's no guarantee of success, strategic risk can lead to far greater rewards. Instead of being afraid of risk, Fastlaners embrace it, knowing that calculated risks often lead to exponential growth.

The Fastlane Mindset: Think Big, Act Bold

To succeed in the Fastlane, you must adopt a new mindset—one that challenges conventional thinking. Fastlaners don't wait for opportunities; they create them. They don't focus on small, incremental gains; they aim for exponential growth. They don't think about how to earn more money in the next year; they think about how to build assets that generate wealth for the next decade.

The Fastlane is about taking bold actions that accelerate your financial freedom. It's about thinking big, acting boldly, and understanding that wealth isn't something you earn slowly over time—it's something you create through strategic efforts.

Lessons Learned:

- The "Fastlane" approach to wealth-building focuses on scaling efforts, leveraging time, and building businesses or investments that multiply your income.
- Avoid the slow path of saving small amounts for decades—invest in high-impact opportunities.
- Success in the Fastlane requires strategic risk-taking, hard work, and the creation of scalable systems.
- Focus on value creation and problem-solving to accelerate wealth generation.

Chapter 5:

Mastering Financial Literacy

At the heart of the Fastlane approach is **financial literacy**—the ability to understand and manage money effectively. Financial literacy isn't just about knowing how to budget or save; it's about understanding how money works, how to grow wealth, and how to make informed decisions that accelerate your financial success.

In this chapter, we'll explore the key concepts of financial literacy and how mastering them can lay the foundation for building and protecting your wealth.

The Basics: Cash Flow, Assets, and Liabilities

Financial literacy starts with understanding the basics: **cash flow**, **assets**, and **liabilities**.

- **Cash Flow:** Cash flow is the movement of money into and out of your financial life. Positive cash flow means more money is coming in than going out, while negative cash flow means you're spending more than you're earning. Positive cash flow is essential for building wealth because it allows you to invest in assets and grow your financial independence.

- **Assets:** As discussed in earlier chapters, assets are anything that puts money into your pocket. They can generate income (e.g., rental properties, businesses) or appreciate in value (e.g., stocks, real estate).

- **Liabilities:** Liabilities, on the other hand, take money out of your pocket. These can include debts like credit cards, mortgages, and car loans. While some liabilities, like a mortgage on an investment property, can be strategic, most liabilities should be minimized.

Mastering these core concepts allows you to build a solid financial foundation. By maximizing cash flow, accumulating assets, and minimizing liabilities, you can create the financial freedom needed to accelerate wealth.

Understanding the Impact of Taxes and Inflation

Two of the biggest drains on wealth are **taxes** and **inflation**. Yet, many people don't fully understand their impact.

- **Taxes:** Taxes are often the largest single expense most people face. Understanding tax laws, deductions, and credits is essential to keeping more of your money. High-income individuals and business owners who master tax planning can legally minimize their tax burden, allowing them to keep more of their earnings to invest in further wealth-building opportunities.

- **Inflation:** Inflation erodes the purchasing power of your money over time. This means that the money you save today will be worth less in the future. To combat inflation, you must invest in assets that appreciate or generate income at a rate higher than inflation.

The Power of Compound Interest

Compound interest is a critical concept in financial literacy. It refers to the process where the interest you earn on an investment is reinvested, allowing you to earn interest on the original amount plus the reinvested interest. Over time, this creates a snowball effect, allowing your wealth to grow exponentially.

For example, if you invest $10,000 at a 7% return and reinvest the earnings, that investment will grow much faster than if you simply collected the interest each year. The earlier you start investing, the more time compound interest has to work in your favor.

The Role of Debt in Wealth Building

Not all debt is bad. In fact, some debt, when used strategically, can help you build wealth. **Good debt** is any debt that is used to acquire assets that generate income or appreciate in value. For example, a mortgage on a rental property that produces positive cash flow is good debt.

Bad debt, on the other hand, is any debt used to buy liabilities—things that don't generate income or appreciate in value. Credit card debt used to purchase consumer goods is a prime example of bad debt. Learning how to differentiate between good and bad debt is a crucial aspect of financial literacy.

Building a Financial Literacy Toolkit

To master financial literacy, you need the right tools and knowledge. Here are some key areas to focus on:

- **Budgeting and Cash Flow Management:** Create a budget that tracks your income, expenses, and savings. Use this to maximize your cash flow and ensure you're consistently moving toward financial independence.

- **Investing:** Learn the basics of investing in stocks, bonds, real estate, and other assets. Understand the risks and rewards of different investment vehicles and how they fit into your overall wealth strategy.

- **Tax Planning:** Familiarize yourself with tax strategies that can help you minimize your tax burden. Consider working with a financial advisor or tax professional to ensure you're making the most of available deductions and credits.

- **Debt Management:** Develop a plan to pay off bad debt and use good debt strategically to build wealth. Keep debt levels manageable to avoid financial stress.

By mastering these areas, you'll have the financial literacy needed to make informed decisions, grow your wealth, and accelerate your path to financial freedom.

Lessons Learned:

- Financial literacy empowers you to make informed decisions about saving, investing, and managing debt.
- Understanding key financial terms like cash flow, net worth, and compound interest is essential to wealth-building.
- Knowledge of taxes, credit, and budgeting allows you to minimize costs and maximize growth.
- Continuous learning in finance will keep you ahead in wealth-building.

Chapter 6:

The Power of Leverage

Leverage is a concept that can dramatically accelerate your wealth-building journey, but it's often misunderstood. At its core, leverage is about multiplying your efforts, allowing you to achieve much more than you could on your own. While many people associate leverage only with financial debt, it comes in various forms—time, technology, and systems—and all can play a critical role in creating wealth faster.

In this chapter, we'll explore the different types of leverage and how you can use them to supercharge your financial success.

What is Leverage?

Leverage is the strategic use of resources beyond your own—whether it's other people's time, money, or expertise—to increase your impact and results. It enables you to achieve outsized returns with less personal effort, helping you grow your wealth faster.

There are several forms of leverage:

- **Financial Leverage:** Using borrowed money to acquire assets that generate income or appreciate in value.
- **Time Leverage:** Delegating tasks to others or using systems to multiply your time and efforts.
- **Technology Leverage:** Using technology to automate tasks, scale your business, or reach a larger audience.
- **Knowledge Leverage:** Gaining expertise and applying it strategically to make better decisions or build systems.

Financial Leverage: The Power of Borrowed Money

One of the most common forms of leverage is using other people's money—whether through loans, mortgages, or investor capital—to acquire income-generating assets. While many people fear debt, when used strategically, it can be a powerful tool for wealth creation.

For example, imagine purchasing a rental property. By using a mortgage, you only need a fraction of the total property cost upfront. As long as the property generates enough rental income to cover the mortgage and expenses, you can build equity and create cash flow with minimal investment. Over time, the property appreciates, and the leverage allows you to control a larger asset for less money.

However, financial leverage comes with risks. If your investments don't perform as expected, you can end up in a difficult financial situation. The key is to use financial leverage strategically, ensuring that the income from your investments outweighs the cost of borrowing.

Time Leverage: Multiply Your Efforts

We all have the same 24 hours in a day, but how you use that time can make all the difference in your wealth-building journey. Time leverage is about multiplying your efforts by using other people's time or systems to accomplish more than you could on your own.

- **Delegation:** By hiring employees, contractors, or virtual assistants, you can delegate tasks that don't require your direct involvement, freeing up your time for higher-value activities like strategizing or scaling your business.

- **Systems and Automation:** Implementing systems, processes, and automation tools allows your business or investments to run without your constant input. For example, an e-commerce store with automated order fulfillment and customer support can continue generating income while you focus on growing other aspects of your business.

Time leverage allows you to work smarter, not harder. By freeing up your time, you can focus on activities that generate the most value, such as acquiring new clients, expanding your investments, or creating new income streams.

Technology Leverage: Automate and Scale

Technology is one of the most powerful forms of leverage available today. With the right tools, you can automate routine tasks, reach a global audience, and scale your efforts exponentially.

For example:

- **Online Businesses:** With e-commerce platforms, you can sell products worldwide without the need for a physical store or large staff. Automated payment systems, inventory management, and customer service tools allow your business to operate 24/7, generating income even when you're not working.

- **Software and Applications:** Software can automate various aspects of your business, from marketing campaigns to customer relationship management (CRM) systems. This reduces the need for manual labor and increases efficiency.

By leveraging technology, you can achieve exponential growth, scaling your income without significantly increasing your time commitment or expenses.

Knowledge Leverage: Apply Expertise for Maximum Impact

Knowledge leverage involves using your expertise and understanding to make better decisions, solve problems, and create value. This can include leveraging the knowledge of others through partnerships, mentorships, or hiring experts in fields where you lack experience.

For example:

- **Partnerships:** Forming strategic partnerships allows you to leverage the expertise and resources of others to accelerate your business or investment success.

- **Continuous Learning:** By continually improving your financial literacy and knowledge, you can make smarter investment choices, identify emerging opportunities, and avoid costly mistakes.

Knowledge is power, and applying it strategically can create opportunities for growth and success that wouldn't otherwise be possible.

The Balance of Risk and Reward

While leverage can accelerate your wealth-building process, it's important to strike the right balance between risk and reward. Over-leveraging—taking on too much debt, time commitments, or risk—can lead to financial strain if your investments or systems don't perform as expected.

To minimize risks:

- Always ensure that the returns from your leveraged investments or systems outweigh the costs.
- Diversify your sources of leverage. Don't rely solely on financial leverage—use time, technology, and knowledge as well.
- Continuously monitor and adjust your leveraged activities to ensure they align with your long-term financial goals.

When used wisely, leverage can be a game-changer in your wealth-building journey, allowing you to achieve financial independence faster than through traditional means alone.

Lessons Learned:
- Leverage amplifies your wealth-building efforts by using other people's time, money, or resources to achieve financial goals.
- Strategic use of debt (good debt) can accelerate growth when invested wisely, like in real estate or business ventures.
- Time leverage means building systems that allow your income to grow even when you're not actively working.
- Leveraging your network and partnerships can multiply opportunities for wealth-building.

Chapter 7:

Turning Knowledge into Wealth

Knowledge, when applied effectively, is one of the most powerful tools for building wealth. In today's information-driven world, those who continuously learn and apply new insights can stay ahead of the curve, spot opportunities, and create value in ways that others can't.

In this chapter, we'll explore how to turn your knowledge into wealth by leveraging expertise, learning continuously, and adapting to the ever-changing market landscape.

The Knowledge-Wealth Connection

Knowledge alone doesn't create wealth—action does. However, applying the right knowledge at the right time can lead to tremendous financial success. This connection between knowledge and wealth lies in your ability to spot opportunities, solve problems, and create value for others.

- **Spotting Opportunities:** The more you know about the world, industries, and markets, the better equipped you are to identify gaps and opportunities. Whether it's investing in emerging markets, creating a new product, or capitalizing on a trend, knowledge enables you to act quickly and confidently.

- **Solving Problems:** Wealth is often created by solving problems. When you understand a market's needs, challenges, and pain points, you can create solutions that add value to others' lives, which translates into financial gain.

Continuous Learning: Stay Ahead of the Curve

The most successful individuals are lifelong learners. They understand that markets, industries, and technologies are constantly evolving, and staying informed is crucial to remaining competitive. This means continuously expanding your knowledge base, learning from failures, and adapting to new information.

- **Market Trends:** Stay informed about changes in your industry or market. By staying on top of trends, you can anticipate shifts and position yourself to take advantage of emerging opportunities.

- **Investing in Skills:** Continuously investing in new skills—whether it's mastering financial literacy, learning to code, or understanding real estate markets—makes you more versatile and valuable, increasing your ability to generate wealth.

The key to continuous learning is curiosity and humility. Don't assume you know everything—always seek out new information and perspectives to stay ahead of the competition.

Creating Value Through Knowledge

Wealth is created by creating value for others. The more problems you can solve, the more wealth you can generate. This principle is especially true for entrepreneurs and investors, where the ability to apply knowledge effectively can set you apart from the competition.

- **Entrepreneurship:** Entrepreneurs who understand their market's needs and apply their knowledge to solve problems can create products or services that offer real value. By focusing on creating value rather than just making money, they build long-lasting businesses.

- **Investing:** Investors who apply their financial literacy and market knowledge can make better decisions, whether it's choosing stocks, real estate, or startups to invest in. The ability to assess risk, spot trends, and anticipate market movements is what separates successful investors from the rest.

Adapting to a Changing Market

The market is constantly evolving. New technologies emerge, consumer behaviors shift, and economic conditions fluctuate. To succeed in this ever-changing environment, you need to be adaptable.

- **Innovation:** Embrace change and innovation. Look for ways to improve your products, services, or investment strategies based on new information or technology.

- **Flexibility:** Don't be afraid to pivot when necessary. If a particular market or business model is no longer working, be flexible enough to adjust your strategy and capitalize on new opportunities.

Adaptability is key to staying relevant and profitable in a competitive world. By combining continuous learning with the ability to adapt, you can turn your knowledge into wealth that grows even in uncertain times.

Sharing Knowledge for Greater Impact

One of the most powerful ways to increase your wealth is by sharing your knowledge with others. This can be through teaching, mentoring, or creating content that educates and empowers others.

- **Teaching and Mentoring:** Sharing your knowledge with others not only helps them succeed but also builds your reputation as an expert in your field. This can open doors to new opportunities, partnerships, and even passive income streams through courses, books, or consulting.

- **Creating Educational Content:** Whether through writing a book, starting a blog, or launching an online course, creating content that educates others allows you to leverage your expertise to generate income. As people seek to learn from those who have succeeded, your knowledge can become a valuable asset in itself.

By turning your knowledge into value for others, you create opportunities to grow your wealth while also helping others achieve their own financial goals.

Lessons Learned:

- Knowledge is a powerful asset—use what you know to create value for others and build wealth.
- Lifelong learning and personal development are essential for staying relevant in today's fast-changing world.
- Identify areas of expertise and monetize your knowledge through consulting, coaching, or creating products.
- Invest in learning new skills that align with high-demand areas for future wealth-building opportunities.

Chapter 8:

The Entrepreneur's Edge

Entrepreneurship is one of the most powerful vehicles for achieving financial independence. By building your own business, you take control of your income, scalability, and financial future. Unlike a traditional job, where your earnings are tied to the hours you work, entrepreneurship allows you to create systems that generate income independently of your time.

In this chapter, we'll explore the entrepreneurial edge —how owning and growing a business can accelerate your wealth-building journey and give you freedom over your time and finances.

Why Entrepreneurship?

Entrepreneurship is unique because it allows you to break free from the constraints of traditional employment. As an employee, your income is typically capped, and your career path is largely controlled by others. As an entrepreneur, you decide how much you want to earn, how fast you want to grow, and what direction you want to take.

Here's why entrepreneurship provides a distinct edge:

- **Scalability:** Unlike a job where your income is based on hours worked, a business can scale far beyond your individual efforts. Through automation, hiring, and systems, you can grow your business without being directly involved in every aspect.
- **Ownership:** As an entrepreneur, you own your business, meaning you control the profits and the future of your enterprise. This ownership allows you to build wealth through both income generation and the eventual sale or expansion of your business.
- **Flexibility:** Entrepreneurship allows you to design a lifestyle around your business, giving you the freedom to work on your own terms. You can decide how much time you want to invest, what projects to pursue, and when to take a break.

Different Business Models to Explore

Not all businesses are created equal. Different business models offer different opportunities for growth, scalability, and income generation. Here are some popular business models that align with the Fastlane approach to wealth:

- **Online Businesses:** E-commerce, digital products, and subscription services are great ways to generate scalable income. These businesses can reach a global audience, run with minimal overhead, and be automated for passive income.
- **Service-Based Businesses:** Offering consulting, coaching, or other specialized services allows you to monetize your expertise. While these businesses may start out trading time for money, they can be scaled by building a team or creating productized services.

- **Franchises:** Investing in a franchise allows you to leverage an established brand and business model. While it requires an initial investment, franchises often come with built-in systems and support, making it easier to scale.
- **Brick-and-Mortar:** Traditional brick-and-mortar businesses can still provide significant value, especially if you operate in industries with high demand or limited competition. These businesses offer tangible assets and can be scaled through multiple locations.

Taking Risks and Testing Ideas

Entrepreneurship requires a willingness to take risks, but those risks can lead to exponential rewards. The key is to take **calculated risks**—risks that are carefully planned and tested.

Successful entrepreneurs embrace the idea of **testing**. Rather than diving into a full-scale business immediately, they start small by testing ideas, gathering feedback, and refining their offerings before scaling. This approach minimizes the downside risk while allowing for massive upside potential.

For example, before launching a full-scale product line, you might test your idea through a small online campaign or pre-order sale to validate demand. By testing ideas, you reduce the financial risk while giving yourself the opportunity to pivot if needed.

Creating Systems for Growth

The most successful entrepreneurs are not just workers in their businesses—they are creators of systems. Systems allow your business to run efficiently, generate income, and scale without requiring your constant attention. This is where the entrepreneurial edge truly shines.

Here are key systems every entrepreneur should implement:

- **Sales and Marketing Automation:** Automate lead generation, customer acquisition, and follow-up through email marketing, social media, or customer relationship management (CRM) tools. This allows your business to grow without you needing to be involved in every sale.
- **Operations Systems:** Standardize operations with documented processes, checklists, and automation tools. This ensures that your business runs smoothly even if you're not present.
- **Financial Systems:** Set up accounting, budgeting, and cash flow management systems to keep your business finances organized and sustainable as you scale.

By focusing on systems, you free yourself from the day-to-day tasks of the business, allowing you to focus on growth and strategic decision-making.

Entrepreneurship as a Path to Financial Freedom

Entrepreneurship gives you the opportunity to build wealth faster than most other avenues. By creating a business that scales, you can generate income without the limits imposed by a traditional job. Plus, you can build an asset that increases in value over time, potentially selling the business for a significant profit later on.

The entrepreneurial edge is all about leverage—leveraging your time, resources, and expertise to create a business that generates income and wealth far beyond what's possible with a paycheck alone.

Lessons Learned:

- Entrepreneurship allows you to create scalable income streams, giving you control over your financial future.
- A business can grow beyond your own efforts through systems, hiring, and automation.
- Owning a business provides both active and passive income opportunities, making it a powerful wealth-building tool.
- Entrepreneurship is about solving problems for others and delivering value, which creates opportunities for wealth.

Chapter 9:

Solving Problems, Creating Value

Wealth is built on one simple principle: solving problems. The bigger the problem you solve, the more value you create, and the more wealth you generate. Whether you're an entrepreneur, investor, or employee, your ability to solve problems will determine how successful you are in your wealth-building journey.

In this chapter, we'll explore how solving problems for others creates value, and how you can position yourself as a valuable problem solver in your chosen field.

The Value Creation Formula

The formula for wealth creation is straightforward: **Solve a problem + Serve others = Wealth.** People pay for solutions to their problems. The bigger and more urgent the problem, the more they are willing to pay for a solution.

For example:

- A successful business provides products or services that solve a customer's problem, whether it's providing convenience, saving time, or improving quality of life.
- A great investment solves the market's need for growth, innovation, or security, creating value for investors and stakeholders alike.

By focusing on solving problems for others, you create value in the marketplace, and that value translates into wealth. The key is to identify the right problems to solve and scale your solutions.

Identifying Problems Worth Solving

Not all problems are created equal. Some problems are minor annoyances, while others represent major challenges with widespread impact. To create significant wealth, focus on solving problems that:

- Affect a large number of people or businesses.
- Cause significant pain or frustration.
- Have a measurable financial impact.
- Lack existing, effective solutions.

The more urgent and widespread the problem, the greater the opportunity to create value and generate wealth.

Innovating to Solve Problems

Innovation plays a crucial role in problem-solving. Often, the most successful businesses and individuals are those who find **new and better ways** to solve old problems. Whether through new technology, improved processes, or unique approaches, innovation allows you to create solutions that stand out in the marketplace.

For example:

- Uber and Lyft solved the problem of unreliable and expensive transportation by creating a mobile app that connects riders with drivers, leveraging technology to deliver faster, cheaper, and more convenient rides.
- Airbnb solved the problem of limited and expensive hotel accommodations by creating a platform that allows people to rent out their homes or spare rooms.

By innovating, these companies didn't just solve existing problems—they created entirely new markets, generating massive value in the process.

Positioning Yourself as a Problem Solver

To succeed in wealth creation, you need to position yourself as someone who solves problems. This could be as an entrepreneur, where your business provides solutions to customers, or as an investor, where you identify companies or assets that address market needs.

Here's how to position yourself as a problem solver:

- **Listen and Observe:** Pay attention to the challenges people face in your industry, community, or personal network. The more attuned you are to others' needs, the better you'll be at identifying problems worth solving.
- **Take Initiative:** Don't wait for someone else to fix the problem. Be proactive in developing solutions, whether through a business, product, or service.
- **Be Persistent:** Not every problem has an easy solution. Some challenges may require you to iterate, test, and refine your approach before finding the right answer. Persistence is key to establishing yourself as a valuable problem solver.

Creating Scalable Solutions

Solving one person's problem can generate some income, but solving the same problem for thousands —or even millions—of people can generate significant wealth. This is where scalability comes into play.

To scale your solutions:

- **Create Systems:** Develop repeatable processes that allow you to deliver your solution to more people without a corresponding increase in time or effort.
- **Leverage Technology:** Use technology to automate or scale your solution. Whether it's a software platform, a mobile app, or an online course, technology allows you to reach more people without needing to be physically present.

- **Expand Your Market:** Once you've successfully solved a problem for a small group, look for ways to expand your reach. This could be through new marketing channels, partnerships, or geographic expansion.

By scaling your solutions, you increase the value you create and, in turn, grow your wealth exponentially.

Lessons Learned:

- Wealth is created by solving problems for others—focus on delivering solutions that provide real value.
- The bigger the problem you solve, the more value (and wealth) you can generate.
- Innovation is key to finding better ways to solve existing problems and create new opportunities.
- Position yourself as a problem-solver in your industry or niche to open doors for wealth-building.

Chapter 10:

The Wealth Equation: Scale and Impact

Wealth creation is not just about making money—it's about scaling your efforts to create a bigger impact. The more people you serve or the larger the scale of your business, the more wealth you can generate. This chapter dives into the importance of scale and how making a larger impact leads to exponential wealth growth.

Why Scale Matters

When it comes to wealth creation, scale is everything. You can solve one person's problem and make a small profit, or you can solve the same problem for thousands and build significant wealth. Scaling allows you to take something that works on a small level and amplify it, reaching more people, generating more revenue, and creating more value.

For example:

- A freelance consultant might work with a handful of clients, charging an hourly rate. While they may earn a comfortable income, their earnings are limited by their time and the number of clients they can handle. In contrast, a business owner who offers the same consulting services through an online platform or hires a team can serve hundreds or thousands of clients, scaling the business and dramatically increasing revenue.

Scaling also allows you to create a lasting impact. The bigger your business or investments, the more influence you have on the market, industry, or even society. Large-scale businesses solve problems for millions of people and leave a lasting legacy.

Strategies for Scaling Your Business or Investments

There are several ways to scale your business or investments. The key is to identify opportunities that allow you to expand your reach without proportionally increasing your time or effort.

1. **Automation and Systems:** One of the most effective ways to scale is through automation. Automating processes like sales, customer service, and fulfillment allows you to serve more people without needing to manually handle every aspect of your business. Whether through software, tools, or delegation, systems allow your business to grow efficiently.

2. **Hiring and Outsourcing:** Building a team is another key to scaling. By outsourcing tasks or hiring employees, you can multiply your efforts and expand your business beyond what you could achieve alone. This allows

you to focus on higher-level strategy and growth, rather than getting bogged down in day-to-day operations.

3. **Leveraging Technology:** Technology can help you scale faster and more efficiently. From e-commerce platforms that allow you to sell to a global audience to marketing tools that automate customer acquisition, technology reduces the need for manual labor and helps you reach more people at a lower cost.

4. **Franchising or Licensing:** If you've created a successful business model, franchising or licensing it to others can dramatically increase your impact. By allowing others to replicate your business in new markets, you expand your reach without needing to manage every new location yourself.

The Wealth Equation: Impact Multiplied by Scale

At its core, the wealth equation is simple: **Wealth = Impact × Scale.** The more people you can serve and the bigger the problem you can solve, the more wealth you can generate. This is why large businesses often achieve greater financial success—they serve millions of people and create massive value in the process.

Let's break down this equation:

- **Impact:** This refers to the value you create by solving a problem or fulfilling a need. The bigger the problem and the more effective your solution, the greater the impact. For example, a tech company that creates a solution for global communication has a much larger impact than a local business serving a small community.

- **Scale:** This refers to how widely your solution can be applied or replicated. A business that scales can deliver its products or services to more people, across different markets or regions, without being limited by the founder's time or resources.

By focusing on both impact and scale, you position yourself to generate exponential wealth. It's not just about creating value for a few—it's about creating scalable systems that deliver value to many.

Focus on Systems, Not Hours

To scale your impact, you must shift from focusing on the hours you work to focusing on the systems you build. Systems are the engines that allow you to scale. They enable you to automate tasks, streamline operations, and multiply your efforts.

For example:

- An online course creator can build a scalable system by developing the course once and selling it to thousands of students without additional effort. The course generates revenue while the creator focuses on developing new content or expanding their business.

- A real estate investor can scale by building a system for acquiring, managing, and renting properties, allowing them to manage multiple properties with minimal involvement.

Systems are the key to scaling because they allow you to increase your impact without requiring more hours of work. The more efficient your systems, the more you can scale, and the greater your wealth becomes.

Lessons Learned:

- Scale is critical in wealth-building—the more people or businesses you serve, the more wealth you can generate.
- Focus on creating systems that allow you to grow your business or investments beyond your direct involvement.
- Scaling your efforts exponentially increases your impact and accelerates wealth creation.
- Building a business or investment portfolio that can scale offers long-term financial freedom.

Chapter 11:

Speeding Up Success Through Action

The difference between people who achieve financial success quickly and those who struggle for years often comes down to one thing: **taking action**. In this chapter, we'll explore the importance of acting decisively, learning from failure, and embracing speed as a critical factor in wealth-building.

Action Over Perfection

One of the biggest obstacles to success is the fear of making mistakes. Many people get stuck in a cycle of overthinking, planning, and analyzing, waiting for the "perfect" time to start. But in reality, waiting for perfection often leads to missed opportunities.

Successful people understand that action is more important than perfection. Rather than waiting until they have everything figured out, they take the first step and learn along the way. Every action leads to feedback—some actions succeed, while others fail—but even failures provide valuable lessons that help refine your strategy.

The Role of Speed in Wealth Creation

Speed is a critical factor in wealth creation. The faster you execute your ideas, the faster you can test them, get feedback, and iterate. This allows you to learn what works and what doesn't, enabling you to refine your approach and scale more quickly.

Consider how quickly markets, technology, and trends change. Those who act swiftly can seize opportunities before the competition catches up. Whether it's launching a new product, entering a new market, or investing in an emerging trend, speed gives you a competitive advantage.

Here's why speed matters:

- **First-Mover Advantage:** By acting quickly, you can position yourself as a leader in your industry or market. Being the first to offer a new solution or product gives you a head start over competitors and allows you to capture market share early.

- **Learning Through Action:** The faster you act, the faster you learn. Every step you take provides data—whether through successes or failures. This feedback loop helps you refine your strategy and make better decisions moving forward.

- **Compounding Efforts:** The earlier you start taking action, the sooner you can begin compounding your efforts. Small actions taken consistently over time lead to massive results. The key is to start as soon as possible and build momentum.

Embrace Failure as a Learning Tool

Failure is an inevitable part of success. The most successful entrepreneurs, investors, and wealth builders are those who aren't afraid to fail. Instead of seeing failure as a setback, they view it as a learning tool—an opportunity to gain insights and improve.

Each failure brings you one step closer to success. By taking action, failing, and iterating, you gain the experience and knowledge needed to succeed in the long run. The key is to **fail fast**—to test ideas, gather feedback, and move forward quickly.

For example:

- A tech entrepreneur might launch a new product with minimal features to see if there's demand before fully developing it. If the product fails, they've lost minimal resources and can quickly pivot or adjust based on feedback.

- An investor might test a new market or asset class with a small amount of capital before committing significant resources. If the investment doesn't perform, they can adjust their strategy and avoid larger losses.

By embracing failure and acting quickly, you increase your chances of finding the right path to success.

Build Momentum Through Small Wins

Taking action doesn't always require grand gestures. In fact, the most successful people often build momentum through small, consistent actions that compound over time.

Here's how to build momentum through small wins:

- **Set Small, Achievable Goals:** Break down your big goals into smaller, manageable tasks. Completing each task creates a sense of accomplishment and builds confidence.

- **Take Daily Action:** Consistency is key. By taking small actions every day, you build momentum that compounds over time, leading to bigger results.

- **Celebrate Progress:** Recognize and celebrate each milestone, no matter how small. This reinforces positive behavior and keeps you motivated to continue moving forward.

Success is often the result of small, consistent actions taken over time. By focusing on daily progress, you build the momentum needed to achieve your larger financial goals.

Avoid Paralysis by Analysis

One of the biggest traps people fall into is **paralysis by analysis**—the tendency to overthink every decision to the point where no action is taken. While it's important to make informed decisions, overanalyzing can lead to missed opportunities.

To avoid paralysis by analysis:

- **Set Decision Deadlines:** Give yourself a set amount of time to gather information, analyze, and make a decision. Once the deadline is reached, take action based on the information you have.

- **Trust Your Instincts:** While data and analysis are important, don't underestimate the power of intuition. Trust your instincts and take action when the opportunity feels right.

- **Focus on Progress, Not Perfection:** Remember that no decision will ever be perfect. Focus on making progress, learning from your actions, and adjusting as you go.

Lessons Learned:

- Taking decisive action is the key to speeding up wealth creation—don't wait for the perfect moment.
- Learn from mistakes and failures along the way; each step forward brings valuable feedback for improvement.
- Consistency and daily action compound over time to create exponential results in wealth-building.
- Speed creates opportunities—act fast on ideas and innovations before others catch up.

Chapter 12:

Diversification: Spreading Your Risk, Expanding Your Reach

Diversification is one of the most important strategies in building and preserving wealth. By spreading your investments and assets across different areas, you minimize risk and create multiple streams of income. Diversification isn't just about protecting yourself from downturns; it's also about expanding your reach and seizing new opportunities in a variety of markets.

In this chapter, we'll explore the importance of diversification, how it protects your wealth, and how you can use it to grow faster.

Why Diversification Matters

Imagine putting all your financial resources into one investment, such as a single stock or a single business venture. If that investment fails, your entire financial foundation could crumble. Diversification ensures that your wealth isn't dependent on the success or failure of just one investment.

By diversifying, you spread your risk. If one asset underperforms, others in your portfolio can offset the loss. In essence, diversification is about balance. It allows you to benefit from various opportunities while protecting yourself from potential pitfalls.

But diversification is more than just a safety net—it's a growth strategy. By investing in multiple areas, you position yourself to take advantage of emerging trends, industries, and markets, all while minimizing your exposure to risk.

The Key Areas of Diversification

To create a truly diversified portfolio, you need to spread your investments across different types of assets. This ensures that your wealth is protected from market volatility in any one sector or asset class.

Here are the primary areas where you should consider diversifying:

1. **Stocks and Bonds:** Traditional stock market investments, including individual stocks, mutual funds, ETFs, and bonds, should form part of your diversification strategy. While stocks offer growth potential, bonds provide stability and income, especially during periods of market downturns.

2. **Real Estate:** Real estate offers a way to diversify outside of the stock market. Whether through rental properties, real estate investment trusts (REITs), or commercial properties, real estate can provide consistent income and long-term appreciation.

3. **Businesses:** Owning or investing in businesses—whether your own or others'—is a powerful way to diversify. Businesses generate income, can scale, and offer the potential for exponential growth.

4. **Alternative Investments:** Diversifying into alternative investments, such as commodities (gold, silver), cryptocurrencies, or peer-to-peer lending, adds another layer of protection to your portfolio. These assets often behave differently from traditional stocks and bonds, providing an additional hedge.

5. **Geographic Diversification:** Don't limit your investments to your home country. Investing internationally spreads risk across different economies and markets, protecting you from downturns in your domestic market.

By spreading your investments across these different asset classes, you increase your chances of steady growth while reducing your vulnerability to economic shifts or market volatility.

The Benefits of Diversification

Diversification offers multiple benefits, but the two key advantages are **risk reduction** and **opportunity expansion**.

1. **Risk Reduction:** Diversification protects your wealth from market volatility, business cycles, and economic downturns. If one asset class underperforms, others may perform well, balancing out your overall returns.

2. **Opportunity Expansion:** By investing in different markets, industries, and asset classes, you expose yourself to a wider range of opportunities. This gives you the chance to capitalize on high-growth areas, such as emerging markets or cutting-edge technologies, that you might otherwise miss.

Avoiding Over-Diversification

While diversification is important, it's possible to over-diversify. When you spread yourself too thin across too many assets, you dilute your potential returns and may find it harder to manage your portfolio effectively. The key is to strike a balance—enough diversification to protect yourself from risk, but not so much that it becomes difficult to track or limits your growth potential.

Focus on a handful of asset classes or markets that you understand well, and build depth in those areas. Quality, not quantity, is the goal when it comes to diversification.

Lessons Learned:

- Diversification reduces risk by spreading investments across different asset classes and markets.
- Diversify your portfolio to include stocks, bonds, real estate, businesses, and alternative investments.
- Geographic diversification provides protection from domestic market downturns.
- Avoid over-diversifying, which can dilute returns—focus on quality, not just quantity.

Chapter 13:

Building Multiple Income Streams

One of the hallmarks of financial independence is having multiple income streams. Relying on just one source of income, such as a job, leaves you vulnerable to economic downturns, job loss, or unexpected expenses. Building multiple income streams creates security, stability, and the opportunity to grow your wealth faster.

This chapter will show you how to create diverse income streams—both active and passive—that support your financial goals and lead to true freedom.

The Importance of Multiple Income Streams

Relying solely on a single source of income, such as a paycheck, puts your financial future at risk. If something happens to that source—whether it's losing your job, a business failure, or an economic downturn—your entire livelihood is affected. Multiple income streams provide a buffer against these risks.

Having multiple income streams also accelerates wealth creation. Each stream of income adds to your financial foundation, giving you more resources to reinvest, save, or use to pursue new opportunities.

Types of Income Streams

There are two primary types of income streams: **active** and **passive.** A well-rounded financial plan includes a combination of both.

- **Active Income:** Active income is the money you earn through your work or business. This includes your salary, hourly wages, or income from freelancing or consulting. Active income requires your time and effort, but it's often the starting point for building additional income streams.

- **Passive Income:** Passive income is income that requires little to no effort to maintain once it's established. This can include rental income, dividends from investments, royalties from intellectual property, or income from automated businesses. Passive income is the key to financial independence, as it allows you to earn money even when you're not actively working.

Creating Passive Income Streams

The ultimate goal for most people is to generate enough passive income to cover their living expenses, allowing them to pursue their passions, travel, or focus on personal growth. Here are some effective ways to build passive income streams:

1. **Real Estate Investing:** Rental properties, real estate crowdfunding, and REITs offer ways to generate passive income through real estate. With proper management, rental properties can provide consistent cash flow while appreciating over time.

2. **Dividend Stocks:** Investing in dividend-paying stocks is an easy way to generate passive income. Companies that pay dividends distribute a portion of their profits to shareholders regularly, providing a steady income stream without requiring you to sell your shares.

3. **Online Businesses and E-Commerce:** Automated online businesses, such as dropshipping stores, affiliate marketing websites, or digital products, can generate income with minimal ongoing effort once they're set up.

4. **Peer-to-Peer Lending:** Peer-to-peer lending platforms allow you to lend money to individuals or small businesses in exchange for interest payments. While this carries some risk, it can also provide attractive returns and consistent cash flow.

5. **Royalties from Intellectual Property:** If you've written a book, created a course, or developed software, you can earn royalties or licensing fees from your intellectual property. This allows you to generate income from your creative work over time without additional effort.

Balancing Active and Passive Income

While passive income is the ideal goal, most people start with active income. The key is to use your active income to invest in assets that generate passive income over time. This might mean investing in real estate, stocks, or starting a side business that eventually becomes automated.

For example, you could take a portion of your salary and invest it in dividend stocks or use your freelance income to buy rental properties. Over time, as your passive income streams grow, you can reduce your reliance on active income, giving you more financial freedom.

Turning Active Income into Passive Income

One of the most effective ways to achieve financial independence is by turning your active income into passive income. This requires discipline and a focus on long-term wealth-building.

Here's how to do it:

- **Save and Invest:** Instead of spending all of your active income, save a portion and invest it in assets that generate passive income, such as real estate or dividend stocks.

- **Automate Your Business:** If you run a business, focus on creating systems that allow the business to run without your constant involvement. This could mean hiring employees, outsourcing tasks, or using technology to automate operations.

- **Reinvest Passive Income:** Once your passive income streams start generating cash flow, reinvest that money into additional income-generating assets. This creates a compounding effect, where your wealth grows faster over time.

By building multiple income streams, you create a financial safety net and give yourself the freedom to live life on your own terms. The key is to start with what you have, build gradually, and reinvest your earnings to create more income over time.

Lessons Learned:

- Relying on a single income stream is risky—building multiple income streams provides financial security and growth.
- Develop both active and passive income streams to balance short-term income with long-term financial independence.
- Real estate, dividends, and automated businesses are powerful passive income generators.
- Reinvest your income from one stream to build additional streams, creating compounding wealth over time.

Chapter 14:

Wealth Preservation: Protecting What You've Built

Building wealth is only part of the equation—protecting and preserving that wealth is equally important. Without proper strategies in place, your hard-earned wealth can be eroded by taxes, inflation, poor investments, or unforeseen events. In this chapter, we'll explore key tactics for preserving your wealth so that it continues to grow and serve you long into the future.

The Importance of Wealth Preservation

Many people focus solely on building wealth, without considering how to protect it. However, wealth preservation is critical because, without it, your financial security could be at risk. Whether due to market downturns, legal issues, or poor money management, failing to protect your assets can undo years of hard work.

Wealth preservation strategies help you safeguard your assets, minimize risks, and ensure that your wealth remains intact for generations to come. The goal isn't just to grow your wealth but to ensure its longevity and resilience in the face of challenges.

Key Strategies for Wealth Preservation

1. **Diversification:** As we discussed in previous chapters, diversification is one of the most important ways to protect your wealth. By spreading your investments across different asset classes—stocks, bonds, real estate, businesses—you reduce your risk exposure. If one investment underperforms, others may balance out the losses.

2. **Insurance:** Insurance is another critical component of wealth preservation. From life and health insurance to property and liability coverage, having the right insurance policies protects your wealth from unexpected events like illness, accidents, or lawsuits. Consider long-term care insurance as well, which can be crucial for protecting your assets as you age.

3. **Estate Planning:** Estate planning ensures that your wealth is transferred according to your wishes after your death. This includes creating a will, establishing trusts, and minimizing estate taxes. Estate planning not only protects your wealth but also ensures that it's passed down to your heirs efficiently and legally.

4. **Asset Protection Strategies:** Depending on your situation, you may want to explore asset protection strategies, such as forming an LLC or trust to shield your assets from creditors, lawsuits, or other liabilities. These legal structures can protect your personal wealth from business risks or financial claims.

5. **Tax Efficiency:** Taxes can significantly erode your wealth over time if not properly managed. Work with a tax advisor to optimize your investment portfolio, business income, and estate plans to minimize taxes legally.

Tax-efficient strategies such as tax-deferred accounts, charitable giving, or leveraging tax deductions can help you retain more of your wealth.

The Role of Inflation in Wealth Preservation

Inflation is one of the most insidious threats to wealth preservation. Even if your investments are growing, if they're not outpacing inflation, you're effectively losing money. Inflation erodes the purchasing power of your wealth over time, meaning that the same amount of money buys less as years go by.

To protect your wealth from inflation:

- **Invest in Assets That Appreciate:** Real estate, stocks, and commodities tend to appreciate over time, often outpacing inflation. Ensure that a portion of your portfolio is allocated to these types of assets.
- **Invest in Inflation-Protected Securities:** Some government bonds and securities are specifically designed to protect against

inflation, such as Treasury Inflation-Protected Securities (TIPS) in the U.S.
- **Diversify Globally:** If inflation is high in your home country, investing in international assets may help protect your wealth from domestic inflationary pressures.

Long-Term Wealth Preservation: Planning for Future Generations

True wealth preservation isn't just about protecting your assets for your lifetime—it's about ensuring that your wealth endures for future generations. This is where long-term planning and multigenerational wealth strategies come into play.

- **Trusts:** Setting up trusts allows you to control how your wealth is distributed to future generations, ensuring that your assets are managed according to your wishes. Trusts also offer tax benefits and can protect your heirs from excessive taxes or mismanagement of funds.

- **Educating Future Generations:** One of the best ways to preserve wealth is to educate your children and heirs about financial literacy, investments, and responsible wealth management. Teaching the next generation how to manage wealth ensures that they won't squander the fortune you've built.

Preserving your wealth is about more than just minimizing risks—it's about creating a legacy that lasts.

Lessons Learned:

- Preserving your wealth is just as important as building it—focus on risk management and asset protection.
- Diversification, insurance, and estate planning are key strategies for wealth preservation.
- Protect your assets through proper tax planning and legal structures, such as trusts.
- Inflation erodes wealth over time—invest in assets that appreciate or are protected against inflation.

Chapter 15:

The Freedom Formula: Designing Your Life Around Wealth

The ultimate goal of wealth isn't just to accumulate money—it's to create freedom. Financial freedom means having the ability to live life on your own terms, without being constrained by financial pressures. In this chapter, we'll explore how to design your life around wealth, using your financial independence to achieve personal freedom, fulfillment, and impact.

What Does Financial Freedom Look Like?

Financial freedom isn't about reaching a specific number in your bank account—it's about having enough passive income or assets to support your lifestyle without needing to actively work. It's the point where your investments, businesses, or other income streams generate enough cash flow to cover your living expenses, giving you the freedom to choose how you spend your time.

For some, financial freedom might mean early retirement and travel. For others, it could mean pursuing passion projects, starting new businesses, or dedicating time to family and philanthropy. The key is that you have the flexibility to live life according to your own values and goals.

The Components of the Freedom Formula

The path to financial freedom isn't a one-size-fits-all journey, but there are key components that can help you design a life centered around wealth and freedom.

1. **Passive Income Streams:** As we've discussed in earlier chapters, passive income is the cornerstone of financial freedom. The more passive income you generate, the less dependent you are on active work to maintain your lifestyle. Focus on building multiple passive income streams, such as real estate, dividend stocks, and automated businesses.

2. **Financial Independence:** Achieving financial independence means that your income streams (whether passive or active) are sufficient to cover your expenses. This

gives you the freedom to make decisions without being driven by financial necessity. To achieve this, it's crucial to create a detailed financial plan that outlines your income sources, expenses, and savings goals.

3. **Lifestyle Design:** Financial freedom gives you the opportunity to design your ideal lifestyle. Whether it's traveling the world, starting a non-profit, or pursuing creative passions, the key is to align your wealth-building efforts with your personal values and goals. Your wealth should serve as a tool that enhances your life, rather than dictating how you live.

4. **Time Freedom:** One of the most valuable aspects of financial freedom is time. Once you're no longer tied to a 9-to-5 job or actively managing every aspect of your business, you regain control over how you spend your time. Time freedom allows you to

focus on what truly matters to you, whether that's spending more time with loved ones, improving your health, or learning new skills.

The Journey to Financial Freedom

Achieving financial freedom is a journey, not an overnight event. It requires discipline, planning, and a long-term focus. Here are some steps to guide you on your path:

- **Set Clear Financial Goals:** Start by identifying what financial freedom looks like for you. How much passive income do you need to cover your living expenses? What does your ideal lifestyle cost? Setting clear, measurable goals helps you stay focused and motivated.

- **Build Assets:** The more assets you own—whether businesses, real estate, or investments—the closer you are to financial freedom. Focus on accumulating assets that generate passive income and appreciate over time.

- **Reduce Liabilities and Expenses:** Financial freedom also requires managing your spending. The lower your expenses, the less passive income you need to achieve financial independence. Reducing liabilities like debt and unnecessary expenses frees up more money to invest in wealth-building opportunities.

- **Reinvest and Grow:** Once your passive income streams are established, reinvest the profits to create even more income. This creates a compounding effect that accelerates your path to financial freedom.

Aligning Wealth with Purpose

Financial freedom isn't just about personal gain—it's also about using your wealth to make a positive impact. Once you've achieved financial independence, you have the freedom to focus on what truly matters to you. This could mean giving back to your community, supporting causes you care about, or using your wealth to create meaningful change in the world.

Wealth gives you options, and true freedom comes from aligning those options with your purpose and values.

The Ultimate Freedom: Living Life on Your Terms

At the end of the day, the ultimate goal of wealth is freedom—the freedom to live life on your terms. Whether that means pursuing your passions, traveling the world, or simply spending more time with the people you love, financial freedom gives you the opportunity to design a life that brings you joy and fulfillment.

The journey to financial freedom takes time, effort, and discipline, but the rewards are well worth it. By focusing on building assets, creating multiple income streams, and aligning your wealth with your values, you can achieve the freedom to live life exactly as you envision it.

Lessons Learned:

- Financial freedom allows you to design your life based on your values and passions, not just your paycheck.
- Passive income streams are the foundation of financial freedom, allowing you to cover living expenses without active work.
- Time freedom is one of the most valuable aspects of wealth—create systems that free up your time for what matters most.
- Financial independence gives you the flexibility to pursue passions, travel, and spend more time with loved ones.

Chapter 16:

The Mindset of the Wealthy: Think and Grow

Wealth isn't just about what you do; it's about how you think. The difference between those who achieve financial independence and those who struggle often comes down to mindset. Wealth-building requires more than just knowledge or strategy—it demands a shift in how you see money, risk, and opportunity. In this chapter, we'll dive deep into the mindset that drives success and how you can cultivate a wealth-building mentality.

The Power of a Growth Mindset

At the heart of wealth creation is the **growth mindset** —the belief that your abilities, intelligence, and potential are not fixed but can be developed with effort and learning. Those with a growth mindset see challenges as opportunities, failure as a stepping stone, and effort as a path to mastery.

In contrast, a **fixed mindset** limits your potential. People with a fixed mindset believe that their abilities and intelligence are static. They tend to avoid challenges, give up easily, and fear failure.

This mindset stifles growth and keeps you stuck in a cycle of limited financial success.

A growth mindset is essential for building wealth because it opens you up to opportunities, allows you to learn from mistakes, and encourages you to take calculated risks. The wealthy see every challenge as a chance to grow and every failure as valuable feedback. They understand that wealth isn't just about what you know—it's about what you're willing to learn.

Abundance vs. Scarcity Thinking

One of the key differences between wealthy individuals and those who struggle financially is their outlook on abundance and scarcity. People with an **abundance mindset** believe there are enough resources, opportunities, and wealth for everyone. They see life as full of possibilities and focus on creating value and growth.

In contrast, those with a **scarcity mindset** believe that resources are limited. They fear loss, hoard their assets, and often view others' success as a threat to their own. This mindset leads to risk aversion, missed opportunities, and financial stagnation.

To cultivate an abundance mindset:

- **Focus on Growth, Not Lack:** Rather than worrying about what you don't have, focus on the opportunities around you. Look for ways to create value, expand your skillset, and seize new ventures.
- **Celebrate Others' Success:** Instead of seeing someone else's financial success as a threat, view it as inspiration. The success of others is proof that wealth is attainable.
- **Take Calculated Risks:** Those with a scarcity mindset avoid risks because they fear losing what they have. Wealthy individuals take calculated risks, knowing that growth often requires stepping outside of their comfort zone.

Long-Term Thinking and Delayed Gratification

Wealth-building requires patience and a long-term perspective. Those who are successful with money understand the power of **delayed gratification**—the ability to forgo immediate rewards in favor of larger, long-term gains.

Many people get trapped in the cycle of immediate gratification, spending money on things that provide short-term pleasure but don't contribute to their long-term financial goals. The wealthy, on the other hand, focus on building assets that will generate wealth over time, even if it means making sacrifices in the present.

- **Invest Rather Than Spend:** The wealthy understand that every dollar spent on non-essential items is a missed opportunity to invest in assets that can grow over time. Instead of spending on instant gratification, they prioritize saving and investing.

- **Set Long-Term Goals:** By setting clear, long-term financial goals, you create a roadmap for your wealth-building journey. These goals help you stay focused, disciplined, and patient, even when immediate temptations arise.

Overcoming Fear of Failure

Fear of failure is one of the biggest obstacles to building wealth. Many people avoid taking risks—whether it's starting a business, making an investment, or pursuing a new opportunity—because they're afraid of failing. But failure is an inevitable part of the journey to success, and the wealthy embrace it as a learning tool.

To overcome fear of failure:

- **Reframe Failure:** Instead of seeing failure as something negative, view it as a learning experience. Each failure teaches you something valuable, whether it's about your strategy, the market, or yourself.

- **Take Small Steps:** You don't have to take huge risks all at once. Start small by testing new ideas, making small investments, or taking calculated risks. As you build confidence and learn from your experiences, you can gradually take on bigger challenges.

Consistency and Discipline: The Wealth-Building Habits

Finally, consistency and discipline are the hallmarks of the wealthy. Building wealth is not about quick wins or overnight success—it's about consistently making smart financial decisions, day in and day out, over the long term.

Here are some key habits of the wealthy:

- **Budgeting and Cash Flow Management:** The wealthy are meticulous about managing their cash flow. They track their income and expenses, ensure that they live within their means, and allocate funds toward investments and wealth-building activities.
- **Continuous Learning:** Wealthy individuals never stop learning. Whether it's through reading books, attending seminars, or seeking mentorship, they constantly expand their knowledge and refine their strategies.
- **Perseverance:** The journey to wealth is full of ups and downs. Those who succeed are the ones who stay the course, even when things get tough. Perseverance and resilience are key to overcoming challenges and continuing to build wealth, no matter the setbacks.

Lessons Learned:

- A growth mindset is essential for building wealth—believe in your ability to learn, adapt, and grow over time.
- An abundance mindset focuses on opportunities, not limitations—there is enough wealth and success for everyone.
- Delayed gratification is a key principle for wealth-building—focus on long-term gains over short-term pleasure.
- Overcoming the fear of failure is crucial—see failure as a stepping stone to success.

Chapter 17:

The Legacy of Wealth: Impacting Future Generations

Wealth isn't just about achieving financial independence for yourself—it's about creating a legacy that benefits future generations. Whether through financial education, investments, or charitable giving, the impact of wealth can extend far beyond your lifetime. In this chapter, we'll explore how to create a lasting legacy and use your wealth to make a meaningful difference.

The Power of Legacy

Leaving a legacy isn't just about passing down money or assets—it's about passing down values, knowledge, and opportunities. True legacy-building combines financial resources with the wisdom and principles needed to maintain and grow that wealth over time.

The wealthy understand that wealth without education is fleeting. Without the knowledge of how to manage and grow money, future generations may squander what they inherit. A true legacy equips your heirs not only with financial assets but also with the tools to sustain and expand them.

Educating the Next Generation

One of the most important aspects of legacy-building is financial education. Teaching your children and heirs about money management, investments, and the principles of wealth-building ensures that they are prepared to carry on your legacy. The earlier this education begins, the better.

Here are some key principles to teach future generations:

- **Financial Literacy:** Ensure that your children understand the basics of budgeting, saving, and investing. Teach them the difference between assets and liabilities, and encourage them to start investing early.

- **The Power of Compound Interest:** Educate your heirs about the value of time in wealth-building. Show them how even small, consistent investments can grow exponentially over time through the power of compounding.

- **Entrepreneurship and Innovation:** Encourage a mindset of value creation and entrepreneurship. Teach them that wealth is built by solving problems and creating opportunities, not just by inheriting money.

Structuring Your Legacy: Trusts and Estate Planning

To ensure that your wealth is transferred smoothly and effectively to future generations, it's essential to have a well-structured estate plan in place. Estate planning allows you to control how your assets are distributed, minimize taxes, and protect your wealth from mismanagement or legal disputes.

Here are some tools to consider:

- **Trusts:** Trusts are one of the most effective ways to pass down wealth while maintaining control over how it is used. Trusts can be structured to distribute funds over time, ensuring that your heirs receive financial support while still being incentivized to pursue their own financial independence.

- **Wills and Beneficiaries:** A clear and legally binding will ensures that your assets are distributed according to your wishes. Make sure to regularly update your will and review the beneficiaries on all financial accounts, insurance policies, and retirement funds.

- **Charitable Giving:** Many wealthy individuals choose to leave a legacy through philanthropy. Charitable giving not only provides tax benefits but also allows you to use your wealth to make a positive impact on the world. Whether through foundations, endowments, or direct donations, charitable giving is a powerful way to leave a lasting legacy of generosity and impact.

Balancing Legacy with Empowerment

While it's important to pass down wealth, it's equally important to empower future generations to build their own. Creating a balance between providing financial support and encouraging independence is key to sustaining a multigenerational legacy.

Here's how to balance legacy and empowerment:

- **Incentivize Financial Independence:** Structure your estate in a way that encourages your heirs to build their own wealth. For example, you might set conditions on trust distributions, such as matching their earned income or requiring them to reach certain financial milestones.

- **Encourage Entrepreneurship:** Support the entrepreneurial efforts of your heirs by providing seed funding or mentorship. Encourage them to start their own businesses or invest in ventures that align with their passions and values.

- **Teach the Value of Giving Back:** Instill a sense of responsibility and philanthropy in future generations. Teach them that wealth isn't just about personal gain but about creating a positive impact on others and the world.

Creating a Lasting Legacy of Impact

Ultimately, the legacy you leave behind is about more than just money—it's about the impact you make. Whether through financial education, entrepreneurship, or philanthropy, your wealth can create opportunities and positive change for future generations.

As you build your wealth, think not just about how it can serve you, but about how it can serve others—your family, your community, and the world at large. This is the true power of legacy: using wealth to create a lasting impact that extends far beyond your lifetime.

Lessons Learned:

- True wealth-building includes creating a legacy that benefits future generations.
- Financial education is one of the greatest gifts you can pass down to your heirs.
- Proper estate planning ensures that your wealth is transferred efficiently and according to your wishes.
- Empower the next generation to build their own wealth while preserving the values and principles of financial independence.

Chapter 18:

The Fastlane to Freedom: Building Wealth on Your Terms

Throughout this book, we've explored the concepts, strategies, and mindset necessary to accelerate your wealth-building journey. Now, it's time to bring it all together. In this chapter, we'll focus on creating your personal Fastlane to financial freedom—building wealth on your terms, using the tools and principles you've learned.

Designing Your Fastlane Plan

The first step to achieving financial freedom is creating a customized plan that aligns with your goals, values, and lifestyle. Your Fastlane plan is your personal roadmap, guiding you from where you are now to where you want to be financially.

Here's how to design your plan:

1. **Set Clear Financial Goals:** Define your financial freedom number—the amount of passive income or assets you need to cover your living expenses and achieve financial independence. Be specific about your goals

and break them down into short-term, medium-term, and long-term targets.

2. **Identify Income Streams:** As discussed earlier, multiple income streams are essential for wealth creation. Start by assessing your current income sources and identify opportunities to create new ones. Whether it's investing in real estate, starting a business, or building a portfolio of stocks, focus on generating both active and passive income.

3. **Leverage Your Strengths:** Everyone's Fastlane journey is unique. Leverage your strengths, skills, and resources to create wealth in a way that aligns with your expertise and passions. Whether you excel in entrepreneurship, investing, or creative ventures, use what you're good at to accelerate your progress.

4. **Create a Growth Strategy:** Your wealth won't grow overnight. Create a strategy for scaling your income streams, reinvesting profits, and leveraging the power of compounding. Focus on systems and automation to free up your time and maximize your efforts.

Taking Action: Moving from Theory to Reality

It's easy to get stuck in the planning phase—analyzing, researching, and strategizing without ever taking action. But wealth isn't built on ideas alone; it's built on execution. Once you have your Fastlane plan in place, the next step is to take consistent, bold action toward your goals.

Here's how to move from theory to reality:

- **Start Small:** You don't need to overhaul your entire life overnight. Start by taking small, manageable steps toward your financial goals. Whether it's setting up a savings plan, making your first investment, or launching a side business, every step brings you closer to financial freedom.

- **Stay Consistent:** Building wealth takes time, discipline, and consistency. Focus on making progress every day, even if it's just a small action. The compound effect of consistent effort will lead to significant results over time.

- **Embrace Adaptability:** Your Fastlane plan will evolve as you learn more, encounter new opportunities, and face challenges. Stay adaptable and open to adjusting your strategies as needed. Flexibility allows you to pivot when necessary and continue moving forward.

Overcoming Obstacles on the Fastlane

The road to financial freedom isn't always smooth. You'll likely encounter obstacles along the way, whether it's market downturns, business challenges, or personal setbacks. What separates those who succeed from those who give up is the ability to persevere in the face of adversity.

Here's how to overcome obstacles on your Fastlane journey:

- **Build Resilience:** Resilience is the ability to bounce back from setbacks. When things don't go as planned, take time to assess the situation, learn from it, and adjust your approach. Remember, failure is a stepping stone to success if you use it as a learning tool.

- **Stay Focused on Your Vision:** Your Fastlane journey is fueled by your vision of financial freedom. When obstacles arise, remind yourself of why you started and what you're working toward. A clear vision will keep you motivated and help you push through challenges.

- **Seek Support:** You don't have to go it alone. Surround yourself with mentors, peers, and like-minded individuals who can offer guidance, encouragement, and accountability. Building a supportive network is crucial for long-term success.

Accelerating Your Wealth-Building Journey

Once you've established your Fastlane plan and started taking action, the next step is to accelerate your progress. Wealth is built over time, but there are ways to speed up the process and achieve financial freedom faster.

Here are some strategies for accelerating your wealth-building journey:

- **Reinvest Profits:** Rather than spending the profits from your investments or businesses, reinvest them to fuel further growth. Reinvesting allows you to take advantage of compounding, which accelerates your wealth-building process.

- **Leverage Opportunities:** Look for ways to leverage other people's money, time, or resources to scale your income streams. Whether it's through strategic partnerships, investor capital, or technology, leverage multiplies your efforts and helps you grow faster.

- **Focus on High-Impact Activities:** Not all actions are equal when it comes to wealth-building. Focus your time and energy on high-impact activities—those that generate the most value, income, or growth. Delegate or automate low-impact tasks to free up time for what matters most.

Celebrating Your Wins Along the Way

As you progress on your Fastlane journey, it's important to celebrate your wins, no matter how small. Each milestone—whether it's your first investment, reaching a savings goal, or launching a new income stream—is a step toward financial freedom.

Celebrating your wins keeps you motivated and reminds you of the progress you're making. It also helps reinforce positive behaviors and encourages you to continue taking action.

Lessons Learned:

- The Fastlane approach allows you to accelerate your wealth-building journey through strategic actions and scaling.
- Your Fastlane plan should align with your values, strengths, and goals for true financial independence.
- Action is more important than perfection—taking small, consistent steps leads to significant progress.
- Leverage your assets, time, and network to scale your income streams and reach financial freedom faster.

Chapter 19:

Your Wealth Accelerator: Moving Forward with Confidence

As we conclude this journey, it's time to reflect on everything you've learned and apply it to your wealth-building path. The tools, strategies, and mindset discussed in this book are designed to accelerate your financial success and help you achieve freedom on your terms.

This final chapter will serve as a call to action—a reminder that your journey doesn't end here. Armed with knowledge and confidence, you have everything you need to create the financial future you've always dreamed of.

Embrace the Wealth Accelerator Mindset

The key to long-term wealth is adopting a mindset that prioritizes growth, resilience, and adaptability. As you move forward, continue to cultivate the wealth-building habits you've learned:

- **Think Long-Term:** Wealth is not built in a day, but it is built daily. Focus on long-term growth, reinvest in your future, and avoid the temptation to chase short-term gains.

- **Take Consistent Action:** The most successful people are those who take action consistently, regardless of setbacks or challenges. Build daily habits that move you closer to your financial goals, and don't be afraid to step outside your comfort zone.

- **Remain Adaptable:** The financial world is constantly changing, and the ability to adapt is crucial. Stay informed, continue learning, and be willing to pivot when necessary.

The Power of Momentum

Wealth-building is a journey, and once you start making progress, momentum becomes your greatest ally. The more you achieve, the more motivated you become to keep going. Small wins lead to bigger wins, and soon, you'll find yourself moving faster toward your financial goals.

Here's how to harness the power of momentum:

- **Stay Consistent:** Consistency is what drives momentum. Keep taking action every day, no matter how small, and over time, your efforts will compound.

- **Celebrate Progress:** Acknowledge and celebrate each milestone along the way. Celebrating progress reinforces your achievements and keeps you motivated to continue.

- **Reinvest and Grow:** As you build wealth, reinvest your gains into more income-generating assets. This creates a snowball effect, where your wealth grows faster with each reinvestment.

Living Your Wealth-Fueled Life

Financial freedom isn't just about having money—it's about using that money to live a life that aligns with your values, passions, and goals. Once you've built your wealth, take the time to enjoy it. Whether it's traveling, pursuing creative projects, giving back to your community, or spending more time with loved ones, wealth gives you the freedom to design the life you truly want.

Leave a Legacy of Impact

As you continue building your wealth, consider how you can leave a lasting legacy. Wealth isn't just about personal gain—it's about using your resources to make a positive impact on the world. Whether through charitable giving, mentorship, or supporting causes you care about, your wealth can create meaningful change for future generations.

By leaving a legacy of impact, you ensure that your wealth continues to grow and serve others long after you're gone.

Your Wealth Accelerator: The Journey Begins

Now that you've completed this book, you're equipped with the knowledge, tools, and strategies to accelerate your wealth-building journey. But remember, the journey doesn't end here—it's just the beginning.

Take what you've learned, apply it to your life, and move forward with confidence. Whether you're just starting out or looking to take your wealth to the next level, you have the power to create financial freedom on your terms.

Your wealth accelerator is in motion. The path to financial independence is yours to travel—seize it.

Lessons Learned:

- Consistency, persistence, and adaptability are key to long-term wealth-building success.
- Momentum builds wealth faster—small wins lead to bigger results over time.
- Reinvest profits and continue growing your income streams to accelerate financial independence.
- Financial freedom allows you to create a life of purpose, impact, and fulfillment—design your life around the wealth you've built.

Thank You for Reading!

I hope *The Wealth Accelerator: From Financial Literacy to Fastlane Freedom* has provided you with valuable insights and inspiration for your financial journey. Your thoughts and feedback mean a lot to me.

If you found this book helpful, I would be incredibly grateful if you could take a few moments to leave a review on Amazon. Your review not only helps other readers discover this book but also supports my work as an author.

Thank you for your time, and I wish you every success on your path to financial freedom!

Warm regards,
Jonathan Cross

www.ingramcontent.com/pod-product-compliance
Lightning Source LLC
Chambersburg PA
CBHW071452220526
45472CB00003B/774